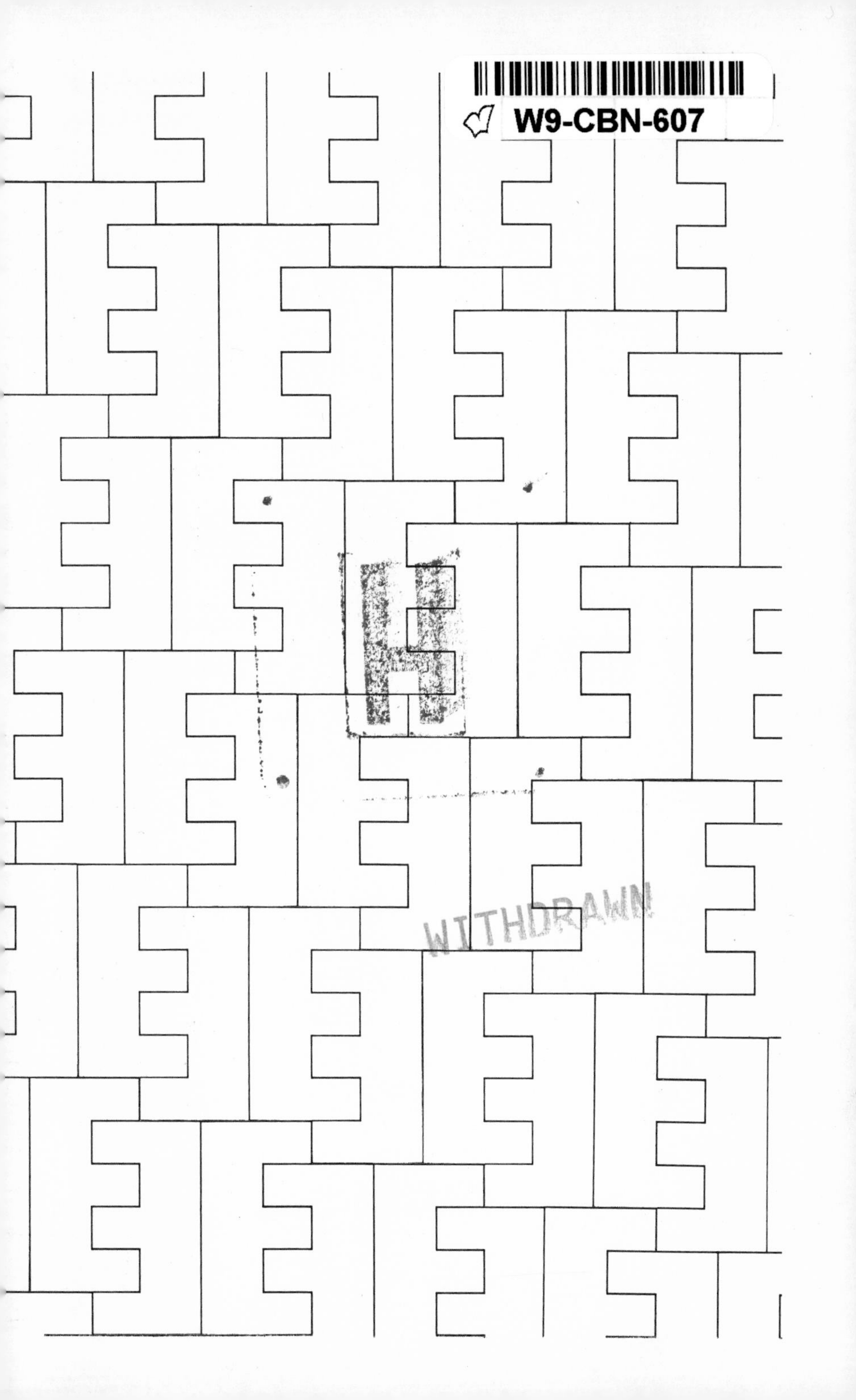
W9-CBN-607
WITHDRAWN

# BOOKS *by Paul Engle*

*American Song*

*Break the Heart's Anger*

*Corn*

*Worn Earth*

*Always the Land*

*West of Midnight*

*American Child*

*The Word of Love*

*Poems in Praise*

*Golden Child*
*libretto for an opera*
*composed by Philip Bezanson*

*An Old-Fashioned Christmas*

*A Woman Unashamed and Other Poems*

*Embrace*

EDITOR OF:

*Midland*

*O. Henry Prize Stories*

*On Creative Writing*

*Poet's Choice*
*with Joseph Langland*

*Reading Modern Poetry*
*with Warren Carrier*

*Embrace*

# *Embrace*

*SELECTED LOVE POEMS*

*by Paul Engle*

*RANDOM HOUSE NEW YORK*

*First Printing*


*Acknowledgment is hereby made*
*to Yale University Press for permission*
*to reprint "These Are the Things"*
*from* Worn Earth. *"You Were Wrong" was*
*published under the title "Mary" by Doubleday & Company, Inc.*
*in* American Song. *Copyright 1934 by Doubleday & Company, Inc.*


*Published in the United States*
*by Random House, Inc., New York,*
*and simultaneously in Canada*
*by Random House of Canada Limited, Toronto.*

*Library of Congress Catalog Card Number: 69–16408*
*Manufactured in the United States of America*

*by The Kingsport Press, Inc.*

*Designed by Andrew Roberts*

TO LOVE:

OUR DOOM AND OUR DELIGHT

# *Contents*


*3* NIGHT SCENE

*5* BABE RUTH

*6* THE WEARING ROUGH

*7* YOU WERE WRONG

*8* CHAMELEON

*10* WOMAN AND MAN

*11* PLUM

*12* TOGETHER

*13* VOYAGE

*14* THESE ARE THE THINGS

*15* HERO

*18* DOG

*19* PARACHUTIST

*20* ROBBER

*21* CONTINENT

22 A MODERN ROMANCE

*26* MOVING IN

*27* FACE

*28* LIGHT

*29* ALL THE WOMAN

*30* FOSSIL

*33* AGAINST THE NIGHT

35 FELON
36 COLETTE
39 TRANCE
40 A WOMAN IN HER GRACE
41 TWENTY BELOW
42 ATOM
43 FIGHT
44 BEASTS
47 ON THE BIRTH OF A CHILD
48 MORNING TO MIDNIGHT
49 YOU
50 MUSEUM
51 EXTREME
52 BARK AND ICE

## *New Poems*

55 BIRD IS NOT ONLY FEATHER
56 BY LOVE WE GROW
57 OUR DREAD TO SPEAK OUR LOVE
58 YOU CAME FROM THE TEAR-SALTED OCEAN

## *A Woman Unashamed*

61 NOTES
62 PARTY

63 WATER COLOR
64 LIGHTNING
65 GOING AWAY
66 GOOD-BYE
68 LETTER
69 DO YOU HEAR ME?
70 ENCOUNTER
71 THE ENDING

# *Embrace*

# *NIGHT SCENE*

I leave your house, turn back
Away from night's blind black
Toward that pale window where
I see your loved face stare:
Dear dazzle whose live white
In that ecstatic night
Shames the electric light.

You do not know I see
Your eyes that look for me.
You find night empty, stand
And wave your empty hand:
Then, like a child, but slow
As if in fear, you blow
A kiss to the dark and go.

I do not know why such
Brief act without warm touch
Should stop a man stone still
And shake him like a chill

On one warm summer night:
A woman's gesture, slight
And quick as sudden light.

So in that empty air
I fill with rage that there
I left the wonder of
Your silhouetted love:
Bewilderment of eye
More passionate than cry
Where touching lovers lie.

## *BABE RUTH*

While Babe Ruth hit those homers I was a kid
Staggering up to the plate in my own bold stance:
Smile, feet wide, swinging the way he did,
Swaggering Babe, whose shoulders leapt in a dance.
June, when a diamond glittered the vacant lot,
Gang with me, bare feet or spikes, too scared to spit:
Noon, the ninth, I'm up, hearing the hot
Clang of the crowd yelling—*Hit, kid, hit!*

Pitch—a pop fly to short—I throw my bat,
Smugger than ever, playing the crowd, salt
Itch of the sweat of shame on my hands. I spat.
Fanning the air, now, on another bench,
Slugger gone sluggish, my hands in their love's fault,
Planning no pride, merely clench and unclench.

# *THE WEARING ROUGH*

This is not time, this always
Moving of immortal light
On mountain, field and dark
Narrow of night.

Nor is the plunge of earth
Time, its forever fall
Downward in silence, no
Cry or bird call.

Time is the wearing rough
Of the smooth brow, the gray
Gathered in ruddy cheek
By day on day.

Even a simpler thing:
The interval of space
Traveled by my bare hand
Finding your face.

## *YOU WERE WRONG*

You said I would forget you, forget your lithe
Body thrusting the night-black water, lifted
On the long swell of the current, the strong feet beating;
Forget you, brown as the granite-crumbled beach,
Running on the wave-hard sand; forget
The way down river with our paddles flinging
Wild and flashing moonlight.

You were wrong,

For always now I see you, always swimming
With body supple as a diving otter's
Churning a wake of pale foam in the torn
And tideless estuaries of my mind
Where the shy fish of memory leap and shatter
The quiet water, their dark scales gleaming.

## *CHAMELEON*

Chameleon, knowing I am near,
Runs the brown leaf in his brown fear,
Dark as dread and light as light
His swiftness doubles with his fright,
Nimble toe and narrow tongue
Leap with the excited lung,
Long tail astonishes the air
Lashing at nothing, nothing there,
Then jumps to a green leaf that's near

And turns to green in his green fear.
My eyes blink in that altering light
As if his fright were my own fright,
Unwilled and yet aware toe, tongue
Move with my excited lung,
And I am changed in colored air
By his change, live and sudden there.

I have watched you, slight animal,
On the long stalk of daylight crawl,
Letting the languid noonlight run
On hair so burned and quick with sun—
Brown dazzle over your brown face—
It gave that light a living grace,
And watched you, startled I was near,
Leap up in mingled love and fear,

And let your hand, slight animal,
Over my trembling body crawl.
So close did we together run
Touching earth was touching sun,
Change to change and face to face
I moved with greed and you with grace.
Shocked that two could be so near
We feared a love so like a fear.

# *WOMAN AND MAN*

We do not know what plan
Our long-shared years have taken,
Each morning yet we waken
A woman and a man.

No way our living took
Is clear enough to find,
We have not left behind
Quick hand or the loved look.

Still we face each day
Intimate and eager,
Mouth has not grown meager,
Still the tongue can say:

Let memory have such
Passionate recall
That we remember all
Worn life as warm as touch.

# *PLUM*

Bloodshot, bold, in the round face of my plate
The plucked eye of that plum stares back at me.
Left, it would have dropped of its own live weight.
Picked, it glares my green glares back at me.

Rain thirsted the blossom to this ravaged sweetness,
This self-destroyed fulfillment—to be tasted.
Without you, mocked by this mellow fruit's completeness,
I look at my branching body—to be wasted.

Yet the doomed air that lost this gay plum's sweetness
Is the lucky air you breathed, with your red lung.
Now I lift up, I turn, this gay plum's cleanness:
My mouth that takes its flesh took your red tongue.

Famished for you, I grab your gift, my white
Teeth tear green skin that your white hand moved over,
Proving and praising, bite by relentless bite,
Only consuming love preserves the lover.

## *TOGETHER*

Because we do
All things together
All things improve,
Even weather.

Our daily meat
and bread taste better,
Trees are greener,
Rain is wetter.

## *VOYAGE*

Sailing from ancient ports of Word, Touch, Nude,
Our hands like drunken sailors prowled the street,
And that we might endure our landward heat,
Breeze from the harbor blew in salt and lewd.
So we plunged southward to that moment of
The hot Equator crossing with a cry
Like seaward gulls, then slow beneath burned sky
Drifted down languid latitudes of love.

In older times men blessed the embarking ship
With wine and prayer and the uplifted hand
Against the sea-rage on the reckless trip.
Reverse for us, resting, returned, who found,
After marine motion, on solid ground
The violence of voyage bless the land.

## *THESE ARE THE THINGS*

These are the things we saw: the wings
Of crumpled butterflies in rain,
Gray lichens clinging to a stone,
Dull goldenrod along a lane.

These are the things we heard: the drone
Of bees in crimson hollyhocks,
Crows in a willow tree, and wind
Rustling the leaves of corn in shocks.

These are the things we touched: the smooth
Wood of worn steps, soft wheel-ground dust
Along a road, a strand of wire
Rough with the rotting of slow rust.

All these you will remember, now
Summer is past and the wind cool,
As long as silver rings flow out
From stones dropped in a silent pool.

## *HERO*

I

I have heard the horn of Roland goldly screaming
In the petty Pyrenees of the inner ear
And seen the frightful Saracens of fear
Pour from the passes, fought them, brave in dreaming.

But waked, and heard my own voice tinly screaming
In the whorled and whirling valleys of the ear,
And beat the savage bed back in my fear,
And crawled, unheroed, down those cliffs of dreaming.

II

I have ridden with Hannibal in the mountain dusk,
Watching the drivers yell the doomed and gray
Elephants over the trumpeting Alps, gone gay
With snow vivid on peaks, on the ivory tusk.

But waked, and found myself in the vivid dusk
Plunging the deep and icy floor, gone gray
With bellowing shapes of morning, and the gay
Sunshaft through me like an ivory tusk.

III

I have smiled on the platform, hearing without shame
The crowd scream out my praise, I, the new star,

Handsome, disparaging my bloody scar,
Yet turning its curve to the light when they called my name.

But waked, and the empty window sneered my name,
The sky bled, drop by golden drop, each star,
The curved moon glittered like a sickle's scar,
The night wind called with its gentle voices: *Shame!*

IV

I have climbed the secret balcony, on the floor
Lain with the lady, drunk the passionate wine,
Found, beneath the green, lewd-smelling vine,
Love open to me like a waiting door.

But waked to delirious shadows on the door,
Found, while my stomach staggered with sour wine,
Green drunkenness creep on me like a vine,
And puked my passion on the bathroom floor.

V

I have run with Boone and watched the Indian pillage
The log house, fought, arrow in leg, and hobbled
Over the painful ground while the warrior gobbled
Wild-turkey cry, but escaped to save the village.

But waked, and walked the city, vicious village,
Fought through the traffic where the wild horn gobbled,
Bruised on the bumper, turned toward home, hobbled
Back, myself the house my neighbors pillage.

VI

I have lain in bed and felt my body taken
Like water utterly possessing sand,
Surrounding, seething, soothing, as a hand
Comforts and clasps the hand that it has shaken.

But waked, and found that I was wholly shaken
By you, as the wave surrounds and seethes the sand,
That your whole body was a reaching hand
And my whole body the hand that yours had taken.

## *DOG*

The dog jumps like a toy
Driven by a spring,
As if he knows our joy,
As if he wants to sing.

Quiet and calm we meet.
Restrained by common sense,
We walk along the street.
Dog shames our reticence.

He runs across the land.
We chase him tree to tree,
Laughing and hand in hand.
A dog has made us free.

## *PARACHUTIST*

Grabbing the earth as it falls away from us,
Feeling its cold slipstream and our clothes flapping,
Taut with the terror of nothing at all below us,
Above us and around us, mighty beyond mapping,
We root our hands in the rock and have no time
To think of tonight, or a second day, or a third,
When deep will mean merely the sea and we will have time
To think what words to use for talk of The Word.

Yet all our grip on ground is for that day
When the mouth, not filled with its fear of emptiness,
Can taste the wheatlike sound of truth and say:
We walk on solid love, on that alone,
Still the faith of a man in a man may bless
His face above its blood-secreting bone.

## *ROBBER*

You are the tree I climb
And cannot rest
Till limb by bending limb
I reach the nest.

Robber without remorse
I do not tire
Until I have climbed so high
No branch goes higher.

In fear and joy of height
I take that tree,
But find from root to top
You have climbed me.

I cannot steal when you
Give branch and leaf.
Robber, you rob me of
Myself as thief.

## *CONTINENT*

Traveler through your untracked sands of eyes
Where my feet stagger and the sour sweat drains
(Glare of your glance, loud where the hot light cries):
Raveler out of the paths of your blue veins
Bleeding their way down hills where my hands follow,
Deft and daft for the valley's lower ledges
Leading deep the middle meadow's edges,
Cleft in the darkness with delight's dark hollow.

Continent once, passionate for wild waste,
Now you are taken, I have mapped each part,
Each yawning field asleep in the sun's live flood,
Want intent on love in your wilderness heart.
Now you are shaken, as, in the high pool, chaste,
Each spawning salmon burns with his cold blood.

# *A MODERN ROMANCE*

Come live with me and be my wife
And we will lead a packaged life,
Where food, drink, fun, all things save pain
Come neatly wrapped in cellophane.

I am the All-American boy,
Certified as fit for joy,
Elected (best of all the breed)
Hairline most likely to recede.
My parchment scroll to verify
Is stamped in gold and witnessed by
Secretary-Treasurer of
Americans, Hundred Per Cent For Love.

You are the All-American girl,
Red toe to artificial curl,
Who passed all tests from skipping rope
And using only Cuddly soap
To making fire in any weather
By rubbing boy and girl together.

We are the nation's nicest team,
Madison Avenue's magic scheme

To show how boy gets girl: my style
Succeeds by using Denta-Smile.

How merchandised that ceremony!
The minister was scrubbed and bony,
And all was sterile in that room
Except, *one* hoped, the eager groom.

Married, with advertising's blessing,
We can begin togethernessing.
Before I carry you, my bride,
Across the threshold and inside,
I'll take, to help my milk-fed bones,
Vitamins, minerals and hormones.

Now look how quickly I have fixed
A dry martini (ready-mixed).
So drink to our day, consecrated,
In chairs of leather, simulated.
While you are changing out of those
Nylon, Dacron, Rayon clothes,
I cook the dinner, without fail
Proving a real American male,

Humble, without too much endurance,
But lots of paid-up life insurance.

From the deep-freeze, to please your wish,
A TV dinner in its dish,
All ready-seasoned, heat it up.
Pour instant water in this cup
On instant coffee from a can.
Be proud, love, of your instant man.

Innocent food, mechanized manna
(Except the delicate banana),
Can you endure—forgive the question—
The messy horrors of digestion?

Even our love is pasteurized,
Our gentle love homogenized.

And now our pure, hygienic night.
To our voluptuous delight
Your hair is up, restraints are down,
And cream is patted on your frown.

The brand-name mattress on the bed
Is wrapped in paper like fresh bread.
We can, to make our own campfire,
Turn the electric blanket higher.
We will cry, darling, I *do* care,
In chastely air-conditioned air.

We've read the books, know what to do,
By science, wife, I offer you
This helpful, vacuum-packed, live nerve
(Just add devotion, dear, and serve).
Hurry! Out back I seem to hear
The landlord's Plymouth prowling near.

If this efficient plan produces
By chance (those awful natural juices!)
That product of a thousand uses,
A Junior, wrapped in an elastic
Inexpensive bag of plastic
(Just break the seal and throw away)
From antiseptic throats we'll say:
It was an All-American day.

## *MOVING IN*

Don't wait for the wind to blow you through the door,
If you need help, here is my hand, I said.
Don't let my walking on the hollow floor
Frighten you, only the dark air is dead.
People more than things can fill a house.
Sit by me on these boxes in the gloom,
Here, with our crumbs of living, like a mouse,
While the fire burns the strangeness from the room.

You answered: Something makes me want to hide
In open air from walls where cobwebs cling.
It's here in me and not with you inside,
Neither an emptiness the years have made,
Nor a house bare of any human thing,
But being afraid that I will be afraid.

## *FACE*

This brilliant weather brings your face to mind.
The last I saw it was in such a light,
Luminous, molded in bone, as if behind
Your eyes it was all fine, alive and white.

Always a burning sun will bring it back.
I hold the sight of you in hand and head.
I tell you this before my tongue should crack
With harder saying of the thing unsaid.

## *LIGHT*

Sunset: a cloud the color of your skin
When luminous with river water, bare.
Above, a sky steadily turning blue
That soon will be as live-black as your hair.

Light alters day. Love alters us. We are
The woman and the man each knew before,
But changed by love's abruptness, as a dark
Room burns with sunlight from an opened door.

## *ALL THE WOMAN*

From now on you will be,
Until the waiting end,
Furtive to each stranger,
Fugitive to friend.

Alone and vertical
At window ledge you stand,
Or walk in willfulness
The long, laconic land.

More than with mouth you speak
With movement, now the shy
Turn of head is talk
And the bare hand a cry.

You need no tongue, your life
Is inner and unheard,
Your meaning plain, for all
The woman now is word.

## *FOSSIL*

We walked in that green field
Between the golden bell
Of Sunday morning and
The golden clover smell.

Beneath resisting grass,
Being too tired to climb,
We found in rotten rock
The fossil lost in time,

Stood staring till I found
Power and sense to shove
Inside my coat dead stone
And your live hand of love.

There we were beaten with
Bronze minutes from the bell
That battered our delight
And bronzed the clover smell.

One hour rock, clover watched
Our deliberate climb
Into eternity
Loudly tongued with time.

Out of green water came
The shell that we could shove
Into the glittering light
That was our wave of love

In which I felt your pulse
Beating, red rung bell,
And heard the quiet boom
Of the red clover smell,

And felt along my hand
That shell whose silent climb
From dark seas into light
Shrieked the cruel cry of time

Accusing us of pride
That we in hope could shove
Up from its salty depth
The muscle of our love.

Stroke by brazen stroke
We answered that pure bell,
As red bloom by red bloom
Clover clanged its smell.

We learned from that dead life,
Shell of old shell: we climb
The living earth to learn
That as we fall through time,

Geologist of joy,
Defining day, will shove,
Layer on layered hour,
Our lapidary love.

## *AGAINST THE NIGHT*

Along the purple branch of spruce
And curly
Bark of birch the mountain night
Leans early.

Walking the downward path we watch
Our shadow
Lengthen over the level valley
Meadow.

Heavy and animal in foot
We enter
The waiting wood darker from edge
To center.

Field lying open as a face
Leading
To barn filled with bulging cattle
Feeding.

We find our house and feel again
How sweet

Between the hungry teeth is loaf
Of wheat.

With lamp we drive the black away
Lightly.
Then hide in sleep from fear that comes
Nightly.

Morning we wake to learn how good
After
Our discipline of dread is early
Laughter.

## *FELON*

Lovers are thieves who steal, but without crime.
Not in secret, each in the other's sight
Plunders caress, look, cry, not for one time
But more than counting, not in the furtive night
But candid evening and shameless noon,
Not the abrupt, scared boy with the stolen melon,
But slow delay, damning all shameless soon,
Each one the outraged loser, each the felon.

The pocket picked, the bawling cattle rustled,
These are plain robbery and honest trouble
By knife or gun or fingers lightly muscled.
But love, that mad marauder, reverses living,
Loots joy but leaves delight, making it double,
Tricks and tenders, taking and yet giving.

## *COLETTE*

Terrified of moonlight as a child,
Ashamed, as a woman, of her shameless eyes,
For love in them the hot daylight defiled,
How could she be both passionate and wise?
First marriage meant: dull home, hot tea, admire
The man, his tie, his cutlet, like a boy.
Second: a burnt child going back to the same fire
Where it had been once burned—but with what joy!

What leads us, scratched with thorns, back to the past?
We drag it, bawling like a calloused peasant
Dragging a calf, to the market of the present.
Pain or pleasure, some things one cannot flee.
Woman I was and this at least will last,
For better or worse, a woman I shall be.

A country girl corrupted into art
She threw her stories at the world like stones
That tore the breathing skin from the aching heart
And showed live marrow in the brutal bones.
She knew the buzzing of the summer bee
Flying above the sting-invaded flower,

And knew the anguished wait for the loved key
Forcing the lock, hour after hour after hour.

The bestial id, mad for its bloody meat,
She had endured, for even it could bless
Bewildered human living that could join
The soul's ultimate grovel in the groin
With a sixteen-year-old Burgundy girl's sweet
Religious wonder at her first caress.

An arrow of rubies bleeding at her throat,
And indignation sparkling in her hair,
To a young man, in angry love, she wrote:
You beg, Share my life. But you mean, Take my share.
Like a hanged man cut down in time to live
I fill my lungs with air and say, Good-bye.
You mostly took while thinking most to give.
I love you, but I want to be an *I*.

Good-bye sticks in the mouth like broken glass.
Under the candid lens of this May light
Coal shovel, hearth and tongs, whatever things

We shared once, now glare at me when I pass.
I want my life, yet now the plain daylight
That touched us both, falls on my skin, and stings.

Person, woman, child, her pride she held
Like a thirsty knife at the live throat of men,
And sometimes slashed, but when they bled and yelled,
Put them to bed and nursed them well again.
At eighty, lack of love was all she hated,
Bought violets with their earth-dripping root,
Subtle and simple, she was violated
By innocence, as a young girl by a brute.

Curled up like a tamed animal, she said
To him, Take! I wish I could give you more.
Then more than body gave to his embrace.
When death came, she said, Take! And when the dread
Looking-glass saw the loved face it bore,
The mirror wept, but not the dying face.

## *TRANCE*

I had looked long over the evening sky
When suddenly it became leaf-light and small,
Hovered over the heavy earth, and all
Sound I could hear was one lost mortal cry.
Now, I thought, am I utterly alone,
Watching a world abstracted from intent,
Far from wild war, here I can be content
To handle human anguish as if stone.

Then the sky darkened and earth tumbled down.
I heard that lost cry come from my own throat.
Ocean and land appeared, familiar town,
Poor homes of men probed by ruthless rain,
And I was glad for shared life, not remote
From misery, but marvelous in pain.

## *A WOMAN IN HER GRACE*

Coming toward me across
The darkened, crowded room,
You seem a moving light
Burning through my gloom.

And when you see me there,
You lift your hand up high
As if in feathered joy
You taught the birds to fly.

We meet. You are no light
Or bird, but face to face
You change to what you are:
A woman in her grace.

## *TWENTY BELOW*

Twenty below, I said, and closed the door,
A drop of five degrees and going down.
It makes a tautened drum-hide of the floor,
Brittle as leaves each building in the town.
I wonder what would happen to us here
If that hard wind of winter never stopped,
No man again could watch the night grow clear,
The blue thermometer forever dropped.

I hope, you answered, for so cruel a storm
To freeze remoteness from our lives too cold.
Then we could learn, huddled all close, how warm
The hearts of men who live alone too much,
And once, before our death, admit the old
Need of a human nearness, need of touch.

## *ATOM*

Now the world, fevered by its moral error,
Shakes like men who crouched in the first cold cave
When night stank hotly of the tiger-terror,
Black air white-fanged, not even the fool was brave.
No honest beast we ask now, hunter and haunter,
But cruel, bragging, cunning man: Survive?
Clever in his bright cave of air, flaunter
Of his snarling, terrible atom, not even alive.

Meaning is fled like temper out of steel,
Toughness gone from the unbroken metal.
Back to beginnings—make a mad world feel
Living anger of love, or let land settle
In the original waters without trace,
The bare face of the water be man's face.

## *FIGHT*

Quarreled. Defied. Fought till love's slashed emotion
Bled hate. Each snarled the unregretted name,
Swung silence like a club to smash devotion.
Each took his pleasure in the other's shame.
Rage that grabbed the infuriated face
Bruised by its look the blue and looking eyes.
Hands that had leaped to hands with the nerve's grace
Hung shaking in that air like savage cries.

Anguish so pure becomes an ecstasy
Where hate and love in the same hot voices speak.
That pride of passion burned us—suddenly
The glacier grief crawled down from each cold brow
To melt along the valleys of the cheek
And frozen pasts ran to one flooded now.

## *BEASTS*

That was a shocking day
When we watched, lying prone,
The two trout sidle under
The underwater stone:

When we saw there beyond
The hedge of hardy thorn
The sexual touch of summer
Luring the lifted corn:

When down the slope the two
Running red fox dared
Daylight in their need,
Poised, aloof and paired:

When cardinals from green
Willows, with red cries,
Scarlet scream of bird,
Plunged in our pool of eyes:

For we, merely woman
And man, did not believe
Living things could love
Wholly, and not grieve:

For love had always been
A nimble animal
That could lure innocence
Or lewd on its belly crawl:

By snarl, by sensual cry,
Love lived, but in a cage,
Barred by my own tight pride
And your rehearsed pure rage:

Pride, pride that would not let
Self give up utterly,
Rage, rage that self would give
Itself up utterly:

They leapt at us like fire
And burned us with our blame,
Defied us with delight,
And shamed our human shame.

We have seen animals,
Finned, furred and feathered, move
From their straight courses, curve
Into one line of love:

Fish, fox and cardinal,
Unreasoning and quick,
Proved one and one are one
By plain arithmetic.

They shocked us with their proof:

Those pairs of parallel
Loves that met and merged
Our own fused futures tell:

Each in the other's view—
Two lines of living light—
Will bend through the bent eye
One ecstasy of sight:

Our shattered parallels
Of rigid rage and pride
Will bend in one live length
Closer than side by side.

## *ON THE BIRTH OF A CHILD*

Daring are women who in a time of death
Give, all meaning narrowed to gun and knife,
To will-less, human child first blood and breath,
With so great cost creating cheapened life.
Yet always to the proud and howling plane
A wordless child will living answer utter,
In the frail wrist but membrane-thin maintain
The pulse's powerful and tidelike flutter.

Let the child flourish, let his light eyes float
On heavy air. Let him, waking alone
In a dark house, defy his own defeat,
Taking murderous midnight by the throat
With hands of long and intellectual bone.
In his time let him taste the metal meat.

## *MORNING TO MIDNIGHT*

Light of the morning holds me like your hands.
The sun at noon looks toward me like your face.
Light of the evening trembles like your voice.
The moon at midnight holds me like your hands.

## *YOU*

You are no slick siren in Hollywood,
Flourishing to the camera her bold face,
Nor the tape-measured blonde, having more grace
Than one bare woman, merely mortal, should.

You are the natural person without fame
Whose loveliness they cannot mechanize.
Life is your meaning. Love is how you live.
You are all feminine, and when you give
Yourself to the full shock of love, your eyes
Grow beautiful beyond measure or name.

## *MUSEUM*

We bring our lives into these lifeless rooms
Offering heads and fields and city places.
We walk those fields and streets and climb those hills.
Our living faces view those painted faces.

I look at you, looking at rock, horse, sea,
A nude caressing canvas where she lies.
You see a painted head and I admire
That portrait watching your admiring eyes.

## *EXTREME*

The weary winter falls
Away from hand and foot
It held with chill, and frees
In earth the frozen root.

Down vacant eave and valley
The melted rivers run,
South wind and swallows call,
Come out into the sun.

Mind and hill relax
No longer blown wind-bare,
Like leaves our faces take
The natural warmth of air.

Never again, we say,
The whispering, wild snow
Will drift across our lives
And drag our walking slow.

Yet we live by extreme,
It is the human way:
Thirsty with night too dark
Our eyes drink in the day.

## *BARK AND ICE*

Now does the valley-river
Freeze in its earthen funnel,
The wary swallow waits
Deep in its windproof tunnel.

No more the narrow fish
Leap for the same fly twice,
Cold in blood they swim
Beneath the iron ice.

Boring under bark
In the frost month their burrow
Grub and worm remain
To crawl the fertile furrow.

Being but human, we
Must cold and crying bear
Huddled together in
The hollow cave of air.

# *New Poems*

## *BIRD IS NOT ONLY FEATHER*

Bird is not only feather and the light
Bone, but the furious idea of flight.
You are not only hand lifted above
Head, but the reckless idea of love.

## *BY LOVE WE GROW*

By love we grow both tenderer and tougher,
Teaching us to delight, and how to suffer.
The pointed nail discovers its true good
Under the hammer driving it into wood.

## *OUR DREAD TO SPEAK OUR LOVE*

Our dread to speak our love is like
The overwhelming fear a latch
Has for the probing key, that night
Has for the struck, revealing match.

## *YOU CAME FROM THE TEAR-SALTED OCEAN*

You came from the tear-salted ocean of our quarrel like some new creature rising out of the primeval sea murky with monsters, from whom in the anguished centuries of becoming yourself you borrowed lung or bone or eye. I did not know who it was until you spoke my name, as if it were a sound meaning *love,* the first word you had learned in a new and never-heard language.

# *A Woman Unashamed*

## *NOTES*

Butterfly trembles when the wind blows.
You walk near me.

The dog barks at the loud moon.
When you come to me,
I speak softly, softly,
Until we are silent together.

For two hundred years
This pine tree has been trained to grow sideways.
I have known you only one week,
But I bend as you walk toward me.

That vase of iris,
Silent, blue as your eyes,
Shames these bawling voices.

## *PARTY*

Opening the door
With one foot lifted I stand,
Because your shadow is there on the floor.
I cannot set my foot down
For fear of treading your shadow under my heavy gown.

Can't I just stoop and caress it with my hand?

I look at trees
Without knowing I see them.

But when you enter the room
I can feel
The eye alive in my head.

In the crowd of people at the party
I see you talking to them,
But your eyes are turned away,
Running around the room,
Touching faces, looking for me.

Surely sometimes it is the leaf
Which makes the wind blow.

## *WATER COLOR*

The painter puts two thin lines
On one side of the page,
And one line on the other side.
Suddenly grass grows there!

Between them, a wavering line.
Water is moving!

Your two eyes look at me.
You lift one hand.

Suddenly my heart is growing toward you.
Suddenly I am moving toward you!

## *LIGHTNING*

Under the willow tree in the stormy night
We huddled together
(For protection, you said, and I smiled in the dark).
Our backs ran with water.
The rain was black.
Where our bodies touched we were warm and dry.

Then a shock of lightning,
Gone in an instant, but I looked at you
Moving a little away from me, startled,
And I cried in rage,
Too much light. Too much light!

## *GOING AWAY*

Why does it take so many people
To get each traveler started on his journey?

Why all that shouted advice from men and women
To a young boy whose back is straight with fright,
Who clutches his cheap brief case desperately,
As if it held his life, not just a clean shirt?

What can I say as you leave this city and me?
Shall I urge you—*be good!* How foolish,
Like telling a fish, Don't get your feet wet,
Or a butterfly, Look out for high places.

I give you no advice but my own name.
Your hands lift toward me and I drop it in them
Like a rare fruit brought from a far country.

You simply speak my name. I close my eyes
As if the sunlight spoke, and not your mouth.

## *GOOD-BYE*

Like a dog lost in the streets of a strange city
I walk around this familiar room where my life
Lies scattered over the floor, clings to the curtains,
Stares with haunted eyes
From the sea-deep mirror which remembers your face,
And trembles from the chair you sat in, talking:

"This is good-bye. I will not be back. Good-bye."

Shouldering the air as if it were in your way,
You left, remote in your long bones,
The man whose mouth had groaned on my shaking shoulder.
Your square back shouted round words back at me:
I feel safe now, no longer violated by love.

Bits of me wander in the garden where we walked,
Lost in the leaves, shuddering under stones,

Prowling the depth of the fish-delighting pond.
Wherever you looked, something of me is left.

Did you know that love could tear a woman apart
Like a bomb exploding or a maniac's hands?
It is noon. The glare of light where you touched my fingers
Shrieks in my eyes. I close them like desperate doors.

And when the sun has been knocked out of the sky,
Should I run crying over the grass,
Trying to pick up night with my weeping hands?

## *LETTER*

I wanted to pick the flower
Gay in the sun,
Its petals glowing with light,
But left it there in the garden,
Too beautiful to put in my humble hair.

Your letter blooms on my table.
I do not open it, in fear
It will say you are not coming again,
And I will tear up the roots of my life and die,
Or in fear it will say
Merely that you are not coming until night,
And I, alone in the hard sunlight of noon,
Will cry:
Why are the petals of your hands not here in my hair?

## *DO YOU HEAR ME?*

In the schoolyard down the street
Children are yelling to be thrown the ball.
They beg with open mouths like little birds.

You do not speak to me in this crowded room,
Although my eyes beg you. Merely because
I am a woman, I must not scream out loud.

I howl like a dog inside.

Do you hear me?

## *ENCOUNTER*

Finding you, unexpectedly, in that room,
Was more than a mere woman in love could stand:
As if on a summer day, in the dazzle of noon,
One snowflake fell on my astonished hand.

## *THE ENDING*

Should I not be ashamed
To lie on this brocade-covered bed
Making these terrible noises out of my mouth
Like a shot rabbit or a dog hit by a car?

I have been this way since yesterday noon.
It was precisely noon.
After looking at your posed face looking
Toward that other woman posing by the pond,
I could do nothing but look at my foolish watch,
Steadily ticking as if time were important.

Your face was suddenly swollen
With that greedy smile
You had often smeared on my eyes,
As a black swan,
Graceful in its arrogance,
Will ruffle its feathers to double its dark size.

I looked again at my watch,
Whose tick was a second pulsebeat on my wrist,
As if I had somewhere to go,
As if there were really anyplace I could go.

A distant bell struck twelve times, telling the world
My love had just drowned in the pond.

2.

Sunlight and time dripped out of my eyes.
I saw you suddenly in your full nature,
The tenderly-tended, artificial man,
Bones brittle as porcelain,
Eyes blue enamel baked in your head,
Your face a fan opened to prove
Every line of the false landscape painted there.

Now I weep, in a woman's way,
Less for the loss of love
Than for the revolting view of your weakness,
Naked there in the sun,
The little boy, whining for one more kite.

I cry. I am not ashamed.

And yet this evening, at the hot window,
I felt that the horrible sun had set
Not in the sky, but here on my consumed hands
Still burning from their final touch of you.

*ABOUT THE AUTHOR*

*Paul Engle,* well-known poet and novelist, is a graduate of Coe College, Cedar Rapids, Iowa; he was a Rhodes Scholar at Oxford and also studied at Columbia University. Though his works have usually identified him with American themes, past and present, the current collection of poems transcends the regional and explores love in all its interesting facets. Since 1937 Mr. Engle has been a member of the faculty of the University of Iowa, where for more than twenty years he directed a world-famous creative writing program; he is now in charge of Iowa's International Writing Program, School of Letters. For a number of years he edited the annual volumes of "O. Henry Prize Stories." Mr. Engle has also prepared an anthology of prose and poetry by former Iowa students, entitled MIDLAND.

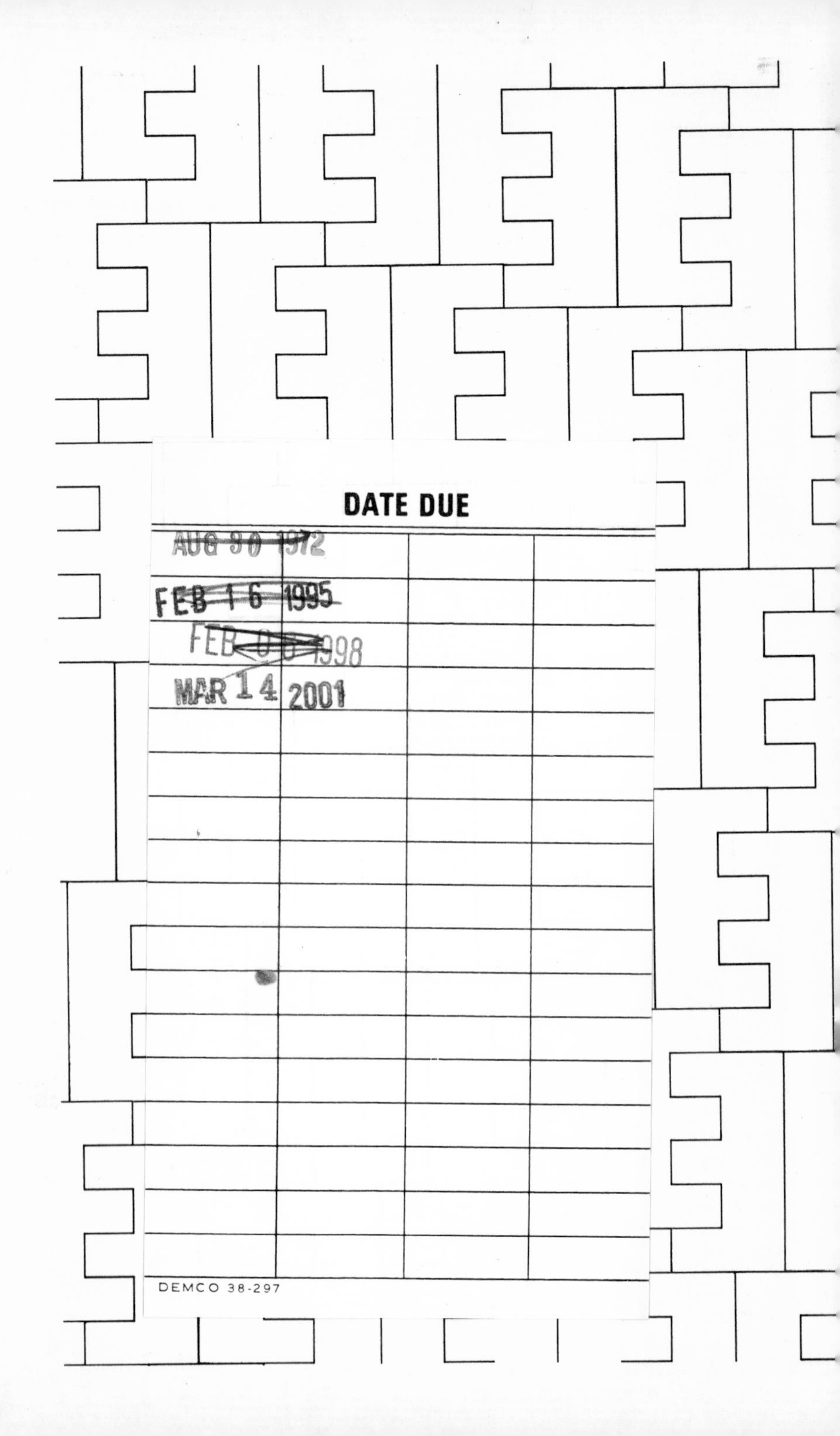